Evincepub Publishing

Parijat Extension, Bilaspur, Chhattisgarh 495001
First Published by Evincepub Publishing 2021
Copyright © Somiya Mohammed 2021
All Rights Reserved.
ISBN: 978-93-5446-028-9

This book has been published with all reasonable efforts taken to make the material error-free after the consent of the author. No part of this book shall be used, reproduced in any manner whatsoever without written permission from the author, except in the case of brief quotations embodied in critical articles and reviews. The Author of this book is solely responsible and liable for its content including but not limited to the views, representations, descriptions, statements, information, opinions and references ["Content"]. The Content of this book shall not constitute or be construed or deemed to reflect the opinion or expression of the Publisher or Editor. Neither the Publisher nor Editor endorse or approve the Content of this book or guarantee the reliability, accuracy or completeness of the Content published herein and do not make any representations or warranties of any kind, express or implied, including but not limited to the implied warranties of merchantability, fitness for a particular purpose. The Publisher and Editor shall not be liable whatsoever for any errors, omissions, whether such errors or omissions result from negligence, accident, or any other cause or claims for loss or damages of any kind, including without limitation, indirect or consequential loss or damage arising out of use, inability to use, or about the reliability, accuracy or sufficiency of the information contained in this book.

Dedicated to

My Soul-Keepers, Maa, Papa & Bhyya

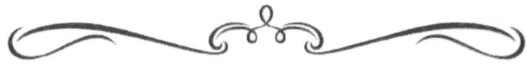

THE WORD COSMOS

LANDLINES

My phone has gone obsolete
it is not fast anymore
it often glitches and
dies without a battery warning.
My friend told me
the average lifespan of a smartphone
is somewhere around two years
and that I should get a new one.
I held my phone close and
checked the contacts
it flickered twice and opened the lists
there lie many numbers which
I haven't dialed since ages
and also, those which I dial almost everyday
but here's the thing
I don't remember any of those.

The first phone in our house
was a bulky ancestor
with a dial as big as my face
it often rang with hostility
and refused to die down
unless someone picked it up.

It had no volume buttons
it was replaced by fancy beetel ones
sleeker, crispier, fancier.
They had caller ID

and options of setting the volume.
They still did not have a contact list
those old phones did not discriminate
they made us remember numbers
they are still etched in some
corner of our mudded minds.

And often,
I am able to recall
the number of
my best friend,
my arch enemy,
the class topper,
my class teacher,
our first mobile phone number,
our second one,
the third one which we bought because
my family thought we needed it
but honestly, we did not.

I don't remember numbers now,
I have them at the click of my finger.
Every single person I meet is a new number
Every person I avoid, is too.

But sometimes I pick up my phone
and my fingers punch in numbers
which I know will never respond
the other end is a deadline
I remember them anyway.

THE WORD COSMOS

The landlines are running low
getting harder to find
they are not really needed
because they could not keep up
with the changing times.

Our phones have become people,
Just like us.

Somiya Mohammed

DO NOT TRUST THOSE

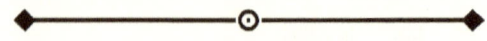

Do not trust those who ask you to fly
before they have seen how deep you have fallen,
who tell you that you can do anything
without seeing you fail a hundred times,
the people who tell you that you are different
ask them how do they define mediocrity
and how often do they indulge in it.
Those who tell you that you are beautiful
enquire whether they have encountered
a body floating on a pond's surface,
bruised with scars.
Do not believe them who come and
tell you that you swept them off their feet,
or they fell in love with you
at the first sight,
Stop and smile, then question them
have they felt pain before?
Or how do they like their morning chai,
How is the sight of parched earth,
or an evening spent in the dark
they will laugh at you, probably doubt you,
ridicule you, even.

But remember, oh dear!
Though you might start your
journey on the road less taken,
it is impossible to go back to your old self

and fall back into the same pieces all over again.

Better make it count!

WHO ARE YOU?

Who are you?
The sickening shade of green on the mosses
or the kind which makes you feel like throwing up?
the trapping black which devours everything
but reflects nothing at all?
The painful red, which stains a white shirt
and evokes a carnal hunger which can kill?
Are you the bland shade of gray that
people fear so much but cannot escape?
Or
Are you the omnipresent nothingness in white
the culmination of everything brought on
one ruined plate?
Sometimes I wonder if you are a rainbow
neatly arranged shades of all the colors people love
but warped in a hundred ways
so that everything loses all its identity.
Interesting it is, how something beautiful can be turned
into something so sinister, so repulsive
when the angles change into bizarre calculations
and that is what I feel when I think about you
You were like a cross, holy and pious
until I realized, I was looking at it
upside down.

TRIAL AND ERROR!

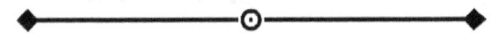

Sometimes the biggest lies are
told with utmost love.
Stars eaten and spit out on the curb
ruing the day
they fell from the sky
ending up in someone's wishes and
then in trash.
Stories written and forgotten,
names carried forward and left alone
to bite the dust.

My red is your yellow,
her blue is his black,
the half is someone's whole,
the front, somebody's back.

Let's play a game of trial and error,
let's find what works for us
and let it go to waste,
Because hey,
that's how you love to play.

WHAT YOU SEE!

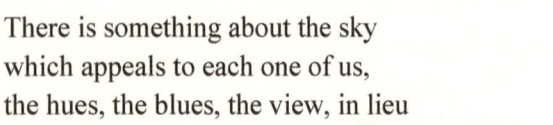

There is something about the sky
which appeals to each one of us,
the hues, the blues, the view, in lieu
of thoughts in mind which with time become art.

As you stare, as you try to recognize the
shapes that clouds make
or
size that moon takes,
you see not what is there,
but what is within.

You see a mirror,
stare at it, blink, think and see yourself.
It is that connection which appeals,
that nostalgia which heals.
Or which needs to be healed?
Maybe.

The creator's pallet has to be special,
it is moody and groovy and has many shades
it has subtlety and poise which never evades,
Yet you see what is within,
Stop. Stare. Blink. Think.

SURVIVING OBLIVITY

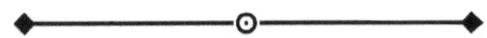

I am who I am
words, tragedies and scars
molded from memories
that remain histories.

I am my mother's laugh
won through days of misspelled grief,
I am my brother's love
dog eared and mishandled,
I am my father's life
his hope for a happier time.

I am that girl who
carved her tears into
words of art then
burnt them just to
keep them hidden.

I am that child
who learnt poetry so
she could have
something to call her own.

I am that woman
still stumbling,
bruised and smiling,

grasping at infinities for
a chance to survive oblivity.

Somiya Mohammed

VICTORIA'S SECRET

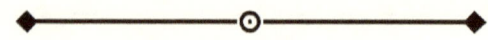

She hides in my room
sometimes in the cupboard,
at times under the bed
I often greet her when I come back home
she is good at ignoring, apparently.

The other day,
I held her hands and told her
it's going to be alright
she laughed on my freaking face
and walked out.

She whispers in my ear when I am asleep
and maintains a check list
of what I ate all day,
when did I take a nap,
how much water did I have,
she walks with a measuring tape and
threatens to strangle me with it,
one day.

She leaves little notes
on the fridge,
on the telly,
sometimes near the bookshelf
almost every day on the mirror
I am getting used to it now.

Last night we had a fight
And I ended up clawing myself so bad
I almost bled out,
She didn't even flinch.

But the other day she did snuggled up to me
when the clock struck 12
and lay silent in my arms
caressing my hair like a lover
who is bound to leave forever the next morning.

Victoria has a terrible secret,
she does not want you to know
but if you hear closely enough,
patiently enough,
she will tell you

She is a lie so beautiful,
you want her to be true.

THE ENIGMATIC LIFE OF A MODERN POET

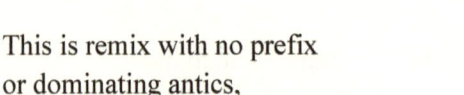

This is remix with no prefix
or dominating antics,
just some word plays with semantic
to show that poetry is not dead
despite the best efforts of a few
gremlins, with too much cred

And there is really no need to give a jolt for
a life reborn or
a brand-new start
where we 'just want to break free'
using words burned in creative hearts.
so, without examination or reanimation
of what could be pulled apart,
bathed in elixir and stitched with
simile like thread,
ensuring words are not too loose,
left to come unhitched,
or each fragment poorly mended
and banished clear from strife,
giving poetry its purpose
and vigor with persistent scribbled life.

Our language still beats strong
with magic metaphoric feats,
allegoric in the sandpit

and our linguistic dancing treats;

This intellectual instrument
a honed and eager mind,
opened up with creativity
with great feelings, it unwinds,
on introspective paper,
with tumultuous spouting page,

And,
if you can't tell the difference;
well, then you are all out of luck.

YOU!

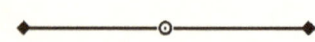

Until I was twelve,
I lived with the belief of
immaculate congruency between
emotions and expressions,
I lived with the concept that
my dad is always happy,
mom is almost always angry,
my teacher is never too tired,
my family is just full,
the world can never run out of life and love,
that god is peacefully resting above.

Until I was eighteen,
I believed I could ace everything,
I believed forever's were a thing,
I believed I just had to flap a wing,
what was life but a big adrenalin swing,
and thence I was living and loving,
past continuous "ing"
all I had to do is to
stick to the right things
turns out, I didn't duck against
the boomerang life was throwing.

Until I was twenty,
I figured life has its ways,
I thought everyone has bad days,
I wanted to believe that it was only when the

storm comes do the trees sway,
rest assured, the serenity stays,
I was grasping for sunrays,
but I first had to live through the grays,
while there is sunshine make hay,
but there is always something
they all have to say
learn to keep the outside happy and gay,
even when you sense gloom
in the bright summer may,
I wanted to sob and cry and just lie
if that was okay.

When I turned twenty-one,
I shunned the idea of
romanticizing what was broken,
philosophizing, reminiscing, writing,
reading, configuring, contemplating, working,
merging mind and heart to one.
Calories to burn,
millions to earn,
families to run,
heart up the sleeve to be worn,
mistakes to learn,
friends to turn,
stories to be spun,
lifetime to have fun,
a future to spawn.

Now when I am twenty-two,
probably still stuck without a clue,
dreams cornered to a few,
I would still dare with all that's strong,
alive and warm inside of me
to ask for,
to hope for,
a sip of chai fresh brewed,
a human by the side to succumb
to nostalgia and go phew!
curse our fates a little and go eeeww,
laugh aloud at the picture of life
I once drew,
staring straight into sky's hue,
shades of blue,
because life isn't a platinum studded
frame to hang from a screw,
it makes you, breaks you, fills you
but the golden rule is
it always outruns you.
It was, is and will be about 'YOU'
the sooner you learn that
better for you.

THE UNIVERSE SPEAKS TO ME!

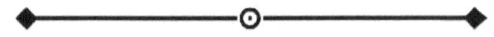

Ever looked up trying to trace it back
when perhaps there was no white no black?
Ever wanted to scream to cut yourself some slack?
maybe it is always lonely down the right track
always been an escapee,
searching for an infinity,
vast multiverse, maybe hiding a deity,
but there is just one for thee,
I am not sure though,
but the universe speaks to me.

Always wanted to glide free,
look for what I cannot see,
yearning to glide through galaxies,
maybe blackholes are the key,

I am not sure though,
but the universe speaks to me.

Plenty of doubts,
plenty of thoughts,
plenty of words,
plenty of ideas never bought,
blabbers all night,
in the void of all light,
it tells me to fight,
that onerous conscience that bites,

Holding up my face,
was not no gloom, not a trace,
dived into those stars we gaze,
all constellations, a creative maze,
thinking about how mankind is a mess.

Seeking wise words from thee,
I am not sure though,
but the universe speaks to me.

Because I love those silences so eerie,
I am quite sure,
the universe speaks to me.

HONOR

Such fragile is our honour
it breaks like a wine glass
holding a cup of milk
to spill around the corners.
The shards remain
for the hungry to be gulped and
puked somewhere else
with their guts out.

Such fragile is our honour
that it refuses to visit our graves
long after we are gone and forgotten anyway.
Such fragile is our honour
that it ceases to exist,
before we could find our way

Somiya Mohammed

STRENGTH ISN'T CLANDESTINE

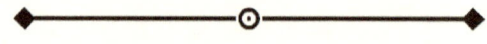

I need no drug to get high,
Oh this life of mine,
is on an inherent cloud nine,
Though with every breath, I sigh
I know it'll all be just fine,
My strength is clandestine,
With a head held high,

My eyes deterrently shine,
But then my hormones are in line,
Blood drips down my throat,
My heart freakishly feminine,
And my stomach just wants to dine,
Ah! People are so imbecile,
I needed this quarantine,
To hear myself whine,

Maybe pamper myself with an ice-cream I buy,
Chocolates and chai,
Good words and sunshine,
Nothing seems to get me high,
some days it's just you that heals thy,
because you know you're not fine,

THE WORD COSMOS

Not all of it is destined,
There are Good lows and Bad highs,
As long as your mind and soul are entwined,
You know it requires spine,
But you'll torch your light, and let it shine.
Baby, you're so high,
Don't need no drug to get high,
You know you won't die,
But this time, don't let out a sigh.
Just like that it'll all be fine.
To the universe,
your strength isn't clandestine.

Somiya Mohammed

YOU ARE THE CONQUEROR AND CONQUEST!

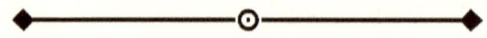

You're the scarred soul and the blistering body,
The blood that shimmers inside
The sweat that glistens violently
As you stoke your demonic light
You're the speckled sky,
The constellations floating in a queer dance
The brilliance of the afternoon stupor
Lit by your inner suns.

You're the veiled earth
And everything that awaits beneath
The breath of its way embers
That smoulder with pulsing heat.

You're the scrawled poetry
The elaborate, enchanting tales
The writers cruel melancholy
That evokes the readers to anguish wails.

You're fluid in a formless motion
An idea rooted in place
A forever that fits in a fist
A moment spanning endless days.

You're the blood-lust of battle
The fury that delivers wars
The dirt that shields the slaughtered faiths
The blood that waters the hopes gone coarse.

You're the ignorance of an innocent
The tinkling laughter of a child
The tightened lips of the guilty
The flinted eyes that once were mild.

You're the strangled voice
The words subdued and quelled
The truth that rises from the bowels
Of the honest, suppressed and ruthlessly felled.
You're the pain of curbed longings
Of love made in flurries haste
You were and shall always be
The conqueror and the conquest.

Somiya Mohammed

SHE LIVED LIKE AN ECLIPSE

She was the sun
and the moon,
simultaneously.
When she entered the room,
the rays of her smile radiated
and warmed the skin of everyone
in her proximity
She was like a light summer breeze
that make the curtains dance when
the windows are left open.
But she was more dynamic than a simple ray of sun.

When she exits the room
and is only in the presence of herself,
the shadows of her soul shake
like flowers after the first frost.
She becomes an earthquake as she goes to war with
her mind.
She was the best of the light, and the worst of the
darkness.
She lived as an eclipse.

YOU OR THE WORLD!?

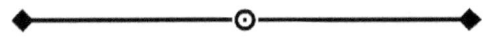

When I ask you some questions
can you always choose an answer
and also tell me why?
sunset or sunrise?
beaches or mountains?
emotions or numbness?

I won't give you black or white,
Cause it's almost always
grey or vibgyor!
because just a life is what we have,
a moment is all we are,
would you rather lend your soul to
yourself or the world?

Whilst you ponder
watch the night sky glitter
stars all shiny and sober,
pouring into you
thoughts as handwritten letters!
seep them in because you must know
that all energy in you
is not yours to keep
you're just a channel
so the universe lets you reap!
Keep it all and you'll choke

Somiya Mohammed

avoid it only to go broke
Scatter it around directionless
your life is then a joke
you got to think it right and
just pull a stroke!

Tell me now
if you've grown up
to put yourself above all,
if you've given up on humanity as a whole,
if you see yourself as a human after all
if you think only you are worth your efforts
but not another soul
if you think alone is a solace,
only to others let loneliness haul

But my friend,
because you've been given too much
you too must give!

Behold the undefeatable stars
lightening up the entirety
with nothing but burning chaos inside of them!
itself on the inside
yet doing its bit
to contribute outside
gulp it down
until sense fits your head
like a crown.

Put aside
the problems you believe
is your boulder,
offer a shoulder,
hold a hand that's older,
be kinder,
let the world wonder how
you
survive a life so tender
because you see it now
don't you?

You are because they are!
and that moment on
your heart sings to you -
TO BE HUMAN IS TO LOVE,
EVEN WHEN IT GETS TOO MUCH
THERE'S NO REASON TO GIVE UP!
Thence you begin to
Love a little more.
Give a little more.
Forgive a little more.
Always, a little more.

Somiya Mohammed

SHE IS ME

In a hidden corner in the universe,
lives a different version of me,
a doppelganger that has the same gestures as I.

I met her once,
in a poetry reading session on Mars,
she wore a brown leather jacket
with black skinny pants and boots,
clearly, looking out of place.

She looked exactly like me, but different;
it felt like I was staring into a mirror that
acts as the doorway to the other corner of the universe.

She didn't read or write poetry,
she didn't know who Virginia Woolf was,
but she knew how fast a bike could go.
she didn't crochet stories from loose threads,
but she could change tires at the snap of her fingers,
and when she looked at her hands,
she didn't see the railway tracks of her hometown,
or the borders that separate us from each other,
or how she used these very hands
to build a world of her own
many worlds of her own;
she didn't see the struggles of the generations past,

or the dance of the love line with the life line,
she saw hands,
just hands.

And while I weaved metaphors out of thin air,
she looked at me like I were a creature of wonderment,
an alien in the country of humans,
a blue bug in the city of red ones,
and she gestured for me to continue,
and I did.

I told the tales of how death crept into my life,
and took away treasure chests filled with my loved ones,
of how weak I had become,
that the load on me was as light as a feather,
and I still couldn't take it,
but I stayed strong, stayed brave;
of how I wanted to leave,
to pause life for eternity
but I stayed, and played this film,
that ends on a happy note, hopefully
she smiled weakly
and walked out of the room.
and I sat there,
reading more poems,
that talked about despair,
and my hands,
and flowers,
and sunsets,
and her.

Somiya Mohammed

LET YOUR WINGS SOAR

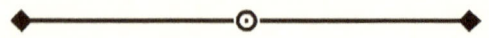

A girl in the mirror with eyes bright
looks my way and shines a smile,
she told of how she left her sorrows in the night,
and has not plastered a mask on her face in a while.

I ask her how she fixed her hair
and how she healed her heart,
she told me she just let it down and did not care
and how her love for herself played a part.

I asked her if she loved her body now
and if she had stopped choking her words down;
she laughed and said to superficial beauty standards
she didn't bow,
she didn't let people get to her anymore
and never abandoned her crown.

She said "I just didn't want to be you anymore"
so, I shed my fears and doubts
and let my wings soar.

VOID IN THE HUMANITY

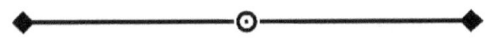

In a hidden corner of the universe
rests an enormous void,
the kind you and I cannot imagine
much less capture in a polaroid,
therein lies the answer to all the unknown dimensions
warped away in space and time and all
the strings capturing our
imaginations imagine a hundred other voids
hidden away in a hundred other corners
of a hundred other universes
in a hundred other dimensions,
imagine being able to move them
over and over again,
with a flick of the hand,
and never knowing that
you have scattered the dimensions like sand.

In a hidden corner of the universe,
rests another enormous void,
the kind you and I cannot imagine
but this, you can capture in a polaroid
and in those polaroid's, you will see
hungry faces amidst swarming bees,
floods that make entire civilizations bleed
and all the idiosyncrasies you can imagine
but you will hesitate,
you will stall all you can

and you will put those polaroid's away
at the farthest corner of the shelf
because this void,
is in humanity itself.

OF POEMS AND TREES

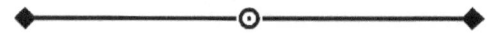

As raw as the bark of a tree,
human emotions shed itself
in the corners of daily regime.
I am not a groundbreaker in any field
but when the crisp brown leaves crunch under my feet,
I can hear autumn trudging its way
into the mood setter called rains.
The place from where I pick my muse
for a poetry isn't dark,
nor a happy place either.

but people here are able to
cry in a social gathering
and pick up their places like twigs
to form a bird's nest.
The place where I buy metaphors
is an ombre palette of overlooked objects
where there is no such thing as too volatile
and people are unaware of the numerical race.
Sins are attenuated in rhymes
and forgiveness is learnt from
the shade of a banyan tree.

On days when I feel blue,
I pick up the lyrics of my favorite song,
sew into a skin that loosely fits my skin
and remain falsely unchanged.

On days when I feel blue,
I look like the leaves of the trees
drawn in a warli painting.

My best friend's mother speaks of *Ayurveda*
and how it requires patience to heal.
I try to replicate the endurance each time love escapes
and my poetry looks
like the veins of dried leaves, astringent.

My poetries leave footprints resembling
the roots of a coconut palm tree,
which typically grows outwards;
the verses follow the process of photosynthesis
in order to synthesize sense out of it.

Agony being the core of all my musings,
I never forget my roots.

IF!

If you're walking down the road
with questions pinned to your forehead
and a burning desire
to lock horns with the raging bull,
You are a threat.

To all those answers,
which were framed without questions
and fed to the people in silence and despair.
They will kill you.

But remember,

before you die,
do not remove the questions
let them pry all from your face,
when you're lying in your open casket
people would see the scars
and gradually

The questions will creep up on their faces too
then we will see
how many caskets they can close
how many faces they can erase?
how many questions they can answer?

Somiya Mohammed

WOULD YOU?

If I asked you to put a finger
on someone who hurt you the most
while you were trying to claw back to normalcy
how much time would you take to
trace the outlines of your face on the bathroom mirror?

If you were to put an identity on your grief
would you use your name, or walk away?
If you were to lean in and kiss someone you love
more fiercely than anything in the entire world
only to die in the same breath at once,
would your lips tremble
or stay quiet like your screams?

If you were given a chance to look at the entire universe
but never be able to tell anyone
for the rest of your life,
Would you take the leap?
What if you died, a little bit
every time you fell in love?
Would you do it?

If yes, I am ready to write an epitaph for you.
If no, I am willing to pen down your lies
along with it.
Let me know.

THE FIFTH ELEMENT

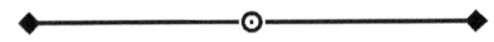

A lion sits in your throat
and a wolf in your tongue
twisting and turning between pointed teeth
a slight hollow under your rib,
right above the liver
you carry remnants of the stake from
centuries ago,

Did you know some wounds trespass generations?
phases of the moon trace their steps back on your body
like a man trying to find his way back home
from the navel to your heart
to the shoulder blades and your neck
fluttering on your eyelids for a moment
And getting lost in your hair
smelling like *khus* on a hot summer afternoon

Dear woman,
Your howl stops the wind in its tracks,
your voice throttles the rage of the jungle,
your body battling thorns like a delicate rose
your arms, earth
your eyes, water
your legs, wind
your breath, fire

Don't you tell me you don't know
that the world keeps you apart
because,
The whole you is a storm
no one has the heart to face.

Dear woman,
You are the fifth element.

THE DAY WE COME OUT OF THE LOCKDOWN

The day we come out of this lockdown,
I hope we come out, not only
appreciative of what was once mundane but also
considerate and aware
of what's been lacking in us.

I hope we tell the coming generations that maybe
binging Netflix,
playing ludo and reciprocating challenges on social media,
will pass your time by all means -
but you'll still yearn
for the satisfaction of productivity
that cleaning your house,
trying new recipes to cook,
using a new pen to draw and
a new colour to paint each day,
will leave you with.
I hope we'll reinvent humanity
acknowledging how much of a difference
our lives and simplest of our actions
make to the world around us,
I hope we never underestimate
or disrespect all those professions
who work for the humanity

in spite and despite of everything.

I hope we'll learn to survive adversities
so when push comes to shove
we will resort to art and books and those old-school board games
and always hold on to the magic of
fingers crossed and wishing at
11:11 to come out of it safe,
spread when the world is not so dope
the lesson of never losing hope.

I PROMISE!

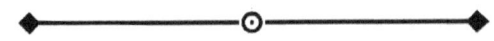

I promise
I'll wear the brightest red on the bleakest days,
that I will hold the fort while you wage a war inside
and I will hold your hand when you are on the brink of
digging too deep in your own heart
I'll take the stabs.
I'll let you in the doors that didn't exist before,
help you crave a window,
let the sunlight burn into your skin and remind
you that you're of the same fire,
I'll burn with you too,
until we become stardust
And return home.

If you wish to walk on the road less travelled,
I promise I'll follow you
and leave little words behind for the journey back
If there's one.
I will take your sins and wrap them in a rose,
everyone is hurtling, yours must be beautiful.
I promise to share the thorns, I'll become the soil.
I promise to be your last-minute rain check when your
anxiety makes it hard to
walk or eat or see or sleep,
I'll help you breathe.
Love saves people and it will save us too,
maybe to the point where destruction is the only

redemption
I promise to stay
I won't become you
But
I will save you
I promise.

POETRY AND MAGIC

Look, poetry isn't supposed to
fix you or rebuild you,
poetry isn't a magic potion that you can gulp
and heal your entire self,
it is better than that
because poetry will hurt you,
it will rip you into tiny little quarks
and it's going to remind you of the bits,
that you are trying
so hard to leave behind till you retrospect things
through the other end of the tunnel so much
that you finally see the way out
and when you read a poem
about something you can relate to,
it is as if it's metaphors and hyperbole
create imagery that dwells in your head
and mess the tassels inside your head more
before these words moonwalk into
the poetry,
poetry is here only to remind you
that your heart is a fragile little thing
and it is going to break hell lot of times
before it finally stops affecting you,
poetry is supposed to do what it is supposed to do,
to break your heart
a zillion times and remind you that
poetry is here to stay,

people,
not so much
and sometimes it is better that way. :)

A letter from me to you!

Hello, You!
So here you are, at the end of the twenty-five poem book which you've just read. Thank you for arriving here with my heart in your hands. Honestly, when I started writing poetries for this book, I wasn't sure whether I will be able to pull this off or not. But today, when I am writing this letter to you, I can totally feel the feeling of accomplishment and immense joy. I would be nowhere and nothing if it wasn't for you.

So, thank you, thank you for choosing **'THE WORD COSMOS'** and bringing it to life. And here I am, sending you love and prayers. May you always find kindness in your heart to embrace people who need it the most. May you find the time and space for the purest joy your soul can experience. May you always shine like the brightest star in the sky. May you keep shining a light in the dark for anyone in need of clearing their visions. Thank you for being you.
Needless to say, I love you!

www.ingramcontent.com/pod-product-compliance
Lightning Source LLC
LaVergne TN
LVHW041557070526
838199LV00046B/2013